THE ENCHANTED TAROT

COLORING EXPERIENCES FOR
THE MYSTICAL & MAGICAL

**AMY ZERNER &
MONTE FARBER**

HARPERELIXIR

An Imprint of HarperCollins*Publishers*

To Ma, Jessie Spicer Zerner, whose great love, art, and wisdom inspires us always and all ways.
And to our dear friend Daniel V. Romer, whose many creative talents we truly treasure.

HARPER**ELIXIR**

THE ENCHANTED TAROT COLORING BOOK. Copyright © 2016 Monte Farber and Amy Zerner. All rights reserved. Printed in the United States of America. No part of this book may be used or reproduced in any manner whatsoever without written permission except in the case of brief quotations embodied in critical articles and reviews. For information, address HarperCollins Publishers, 195 Broadway, New York, NY 10007.

HarperCollins books may be purchased for educational, business, or sales promotional use. For information, please email the Special Markets Department at SPsales@harpercollins.com.

FIRST EDITION

Designed by Yvonne Chan

Library of Congress Cataloging-in-Publication Data has been applied for.

ISBN 978-0-06-256483-2

21 LSC 10 9 8 7 6 5 4 3

Welcome to *The Enchanted Tarot*. As you set out on a magical journey that bridges worlds both within and without, we invite you to contemplate the benevolent wisdom of the tarot and the gentle guidance that it offers. Within these pages you will encounter the twenty-two cards of the Major Arcana—the "trump" cards of the tarot—and the sixteen "court" cards of the Minor Arcana, the "suits" of the tarot. Each card possesses its own special meaning and is designed to embody and convey a mystical message to both our conscious and subconscious minds, using visual symbolism. Together, the images and accompanying wisdom words trigger intuitive associations, uniquely and directly bringing to life the fundamental principle underlying the tarot: the blending of our dream-consciousness with that of our waking mind to produce a state of enchantment. As you contemplate and color *The Enchanted Tarot*, we hope that you will be inspired to reflect on your own personal spiritual journey, and the signs and symbols all around you that offer guidance and illumination.

THE FOOL

DO NOT FEAR–TRUST AND
GO WITH THE FLOW. HAVE FUN.

TRUST

◈

INNOCENCE

◈

PLAYFULNESS

◈

LEISURE

◈

ADVENTURE

◈

BEGINNING

THE MAGICIAN

YOU'VE GOT THE POWER AND SKILL TO MAKE MAGIC.

ENERGY

VISUALIZATION

SKILL

REVELATION

DESTINY

MANIFESTATION

HIGH PRIESTESS

USE YOUR INTUITION—LET IT
REVEAL THE ANSWERS.

SIXTH SENSE

RECEPTIVITY

KNOWING

PHILOSOPHY

FEMININITY

MEDITATION

THE EMPRESS

ALLOW NATURE'S BEAUTY TO INSPIRE YOUR CREATIVITY.

CREATIVITY

BEAUTY

ABUNDANCE

HARMONY

SENSUOUSNESS

BIRTHING

THE EMPEROR

STAY CALM AND FOCUS YOUR ATTENTION ON YOUR GOAL.

ACHIEVEMENT

◆

BENEVOLENCE

◆

LEADERSHIP

◆

CHARISMA

◆

POWER

THE HIEROPHANT

SHARE BLESSINGS FOR COMFORT AND SUPPORT.

TRADITION

AUTHORITY

CODE OF ETHICS

BELIEF

MENTOR

REUNION

THE LOVERS

FOLLOW YOUR BLISS AND CHOOSE WISELY.

ATTRACTION

PACT

RELATIONSHIP

CHOICE

ATTUNEMENT

CONSEQUENCES

THE CHARIOT

YOU ARE A CHAMPION—SEIZE THE DAY!

DETERMINATION

CONTROL

WILLPOWER

GOALS

PREPARATION

PRAISE

STRENGTH

YOU WILL ACCOMPLISH WITH LOVE
WHAT FORCE CANNOT.

BRAVE HEART

◆

DEVOTION

◆

LOVE

◆

LOYALTY

◆

ALLEGIANCE

◆

ENDURANCE

THE HERMIT

SOMETIMES YOU MUST WALK YOUR OWN PATH.

INTROSPECTION

MYSTICISM

◆

ECCENTRICITY

◆

WISDOM

◆

COUNSEL

◆

TEACHER

WHEEL OF FORTUNE

LUCK MAY BE GOOD KARMA, RETURNING.

CYCLES

SURPRISE

TIMING

KARMA

GOOD FORTUNE

LUCK

JUSTICE

YOU REAP WHAT YOU SOW, SO BE PREPARED.

TRUTH

STRUCTURE

BALANCE

ADJUSTMENT

MORALITY

LEGAL MATTERS

THE HANGED MAN

LOOK AT THINGS FROM A DIFFERENT PERSPECTIVE.

SUSPENSION

WAITING

VULNERABILITY

PROCESS

DELAYS

HANG-UPS

DEATH

ONE CYCLE WILL END SO ANOTHER CAN BEGIN.

TRANSFORMATION

ENDINGS

RELINQUISHING

RENEWAL

SURRENDER

TRANSITION

TEMPERANCE

YOU MUST ENJOY THE PROCESS
AS MUCH AS THE RESULT.

PATIENCE

SYNTHESIS

FORGIVENESS

HEALING

MODERATION

BLENDING

THE DEVIL

WE ALL HAVE A SHADOW SIDE WE MUST CONFRONT.

SEDUCTION

GRATIFICATION

TEMPTATION

NEGATIVITY

CHALLENGES

DEPENDENCE

THE TOWER

THE OPPORTUNITY TO REINVENT YOUR LIFE IS NOW.

CRISIS

LIBERATION

FLUX

UPHEAVAL

FREEDOM

RELEASE

THE UNEXPECTED

THE STAR

SURROUND YOURSELF WITH POSITIVE, HEALING ENERGY.

ILLUMINATION

PEACE

REJUVENATION

INSPIRATION

OPTIMISM

PURIFICATION

THE MOON

USE FAITH TO GUIDE YOU THROUGH THE UNKNOWN.

NIGHT JOURNEY

DREAMS

SERENDIPITY

ILLUSIONS

CONFUSION

INSTINCTS

THE SUN

LET YOUR SUCCESSES MOTIVATE
YOU, NOT YOUR FAILURES.

RADIANCE

VALIDATION

LIGHT

SUPPORT

EMPOWERMENT

HAPPINESS

JUDGMENT

LISTEN TO THE VOICE OF YOUR HIGHER SELF.

RECKONING

ATONEMENT

URGENCY

REALIZATION

DECISION

EVOLUTION

THE WORLD

BE AWARE OF AND APPRECIATE
THE CYCLES OF LIFE.

CULMINATION

AWARENESS

GRADUATION

EXPANSION

DISCOVERY

PRINCESS OF WANDS

ACTIONS SPEAK LOUDER THAN WORDS.

SPONTANEITY

IMPATIENCE

ENTHUSIASM

INNOCENCE

GROWTH

YOUTHFULNESS

PRINCE OF WANDS

GET MOTIVATED SO THAT YOU CAN MOVE FORWARD.

AMBITION

IMPETUOUSNESS

EAGERNESS

PASSION

PROGRESS

MOVEMENT

QUEEN OF WANDS

BE INSPIRED BY THE ENERGY OF THE UNIVERSE.

INSPIRATION

◆

ASSERTION

◆

ENERGY

◆

GOALS

◆

CONFIDENCE

◆

SOCIABILITY

◆

PRIDE

KING OF WANDS

YOUR STRENGTH HELPS YOU OVERCOME YOUR WEAKNESS.

DYNAMISM

ACTIONS

IDEALISM

KEENNESS

ANALYSIS

LEADERSHIP

PRINCESS
OF SWORDS

USE YOUR ABILITIES TO COMMUNICATE CLEARLY.

IDEAS

THEORIES

GOSSIP

◆

COMMUNICATION

◆

CLEVERNESS

SURPRISES

PRINCE OF SWORDS

TURN IDEAS INTO REALITY WITH INGENUITY.

INGENUITY

CUNNING

DEFENSIVENESS

AGGRESSION

OUTSPOKENNESS

QUEEN OF SWORDS

THINK WITH YOUR HEAD, NOT YOUR HEART.

INDEPENDENCE

SELF-SUFFICIENCY

ORGANIZED

CLARITY

TRUTHFULNESS

INSIGHTS

KING OF SWORDS

BE A THOUGHTFUL AND FAIR ADVISOR.

INTELLECT

AUTHORITY

◆

RULES

◆

BRAINSTORM

DIPLOMATIC

◆

FORCEFULNESS

PRINCESS OF HEARTS

SHARE YOUR FEELINGS, INTUITIONS, AND DREAMS.

FONDNESS

AFFECTION

TENDERNESS

FANTASY

DREAMS

SENSITIVITY

PRINCE OF HEARTS

IMAGINE AN EXPERIENCE OF TRANSPORTING LOVE.

CHARM

POETRY

SECRETS

EXPLORATION

FLIRTATION

SEXUALITY

QUEEN OF HEARTS

THINK WITH YOUR HEART, NOT WITH YOUR HEAD.

EMPATHY

NURTURING

CARING

CLAIRVOYANCE

KINDNESS

DEVOTION

KING OF HEARTS

BE CONSIDERATE AND COUNSEL OTHERS WISELY.

CONSIDERATION

HEALER

COUNSELOR

COMPASSION

UNDERSTANDING

ARTIST

PRINCESS OF PENTACLES

TRUST YOUR INSTINCTS TO MAKE YOUR IDEAS REAL.

PRACTICAL

HELPFUL

PRODUCTIVE

PERSEVERE

SENSIBLE

COMMERCIAL

PRINCE OF PENTACLES

SHOW THAT YOU KNOW HOW TO GROW.

TRUSTWORTHINESS

RELIABILITY

STUBBORN

SERIOUS

DILIGENT

RESPONSIBLE

QUEEN OF PENTACLES

ENJOY ART AND SHARE YOUR GOOD FORTUNE.

SOCIALIZE

PATRONAGE

INFLUENCE

GRATITUDE

AFFLUENCE

RESULTS

PROFIT

KING OF PENTACLES

BE PRAGMATIC AND SELF-DISCIPLINED.

PRACTICAL

WORTH

PROSPEROUS

EARTHY

GENEROUS

COMMON SENSE

ARTIST'S NOTE

My name is Amy Zerner and I am the daughter of Jessie Spicer Zerner, a master artist whose sublime skill with pen and ink created dozens of coloring books that you, your parents, and maybe your grandparents grew up on. Coloring books are to me a symbol of my mother's love, both for her children and children of all ages. I am proud to continue my family tradition with *The Enchanted Tarot* coloring book, my own labor of love, which we dedicate to my mother's memory. Its art and words are based on the best-selling *Enchanted Tarot* card deck and book set, which I created with my author husband, Monte Farber. Each of the thirty-eight fanciful illustrations in this book is derived from a fabric collage tapestry made from textiles, laces, trimmings, and special embellishments, a technique I evolved so I could create intricate, multi-layered, fairy tale worlds that make every tarot card a magical work of art. My husband and I have dedicated our lives to using our art to make the timeless truths of ancient systems of knowledge and personal power accessible and useful. Enjoy!

ABOUT THE ARTIST AND AUTHOR

Amy Zerner and Monte Farber are designers of personal oracles and divination systems. Since 1988, Amy Zerner, a U.S. National Endowment for the Arts award-winning fine artist, and author Monte Farber, her husband of forty-two years, have created their family of forty-five of what they call their line of "spiritual power tools"—*The Enchanted Tarot, The Instant Tarot Reader, Tarot Secrets, Karma Cards, Chakra Meditation Kit, Goddess Guide Me, The Psychic Circle, Truth Fairy Pendulum Kit, The Enchanted Spellboard, Sun Sign Secrets, The Soulmate Path, Quantum Affirmations,* and *The Zerner/Farber Tarot Deck*. There are over two million copies of their works in print in sixteen languages. Their websites are www.TheEnchantedWorld.com, www.AmyZerner.com, and www.MonteFarber.com.